HIDING in a FORT

Backyard Retreats for Kids

Lawson Drinkard

Illustrated by Fran Lee

GIBBS·SMITH ✈P PUBLISHER

Salt Lake City

For my grandmother Margaret Buch Drinkard,
who encouraged my imagination and nurtured my creative spirit. —GLD

For my husband, Ted Gadecki,
I'll hide in a fort with you any day. —FL

First Edition
99 00 01 02 03 5 4 3 2 1
Text copyright © 1999 by G. Lawson Drinkard III
Illustrations © 1999 by Fran Lee

This is a Gibbs Smith Junior Book, published by
Gibbs Smith, Publisher
P.O. Box 667
Layton, Utah 84041
Visit our Web site: www.gibbs-smith.com

Design by Fran Lee
Printed and bound in Hong Kong

Note: Some of the activities suggested in this book require adult assistance and supervision, as noted throughout. Children and their guardians should always use common sense and good judgment for building and playing safely. The publisher and author assume no responsibility for any damages or injuries incurred while performing any of the activities in this book, neither are they responsible for the result of these projects.

Library of Congress Cataloging-in-Publication Data
Drinkard, G. Lawson, 1951-
   Hiding in a fort : backyard retreats for kids / Lawson Drinkard and Fran Lee
      p.   cm
   Summary : Provides instruction for building a variety of backyard hideaways,
including a pallet fort, lean-to, and a snow fort.
   ISBN 0-87905-865-X
   1. Children's playhouses—Juvenile literature.   [1. Building. 2. Handicraft]   I. Lee, Fran. II. Title.
TH4967.D75 1999
745.5—dc21   98-45270
                                                                        CIP
                                                                        AC

Contents

Dream Spaces

WHEN I WAS A SMALL BOY, I spent a lot of time with my grandmother Margaret. She filled my mind with stories about her own childhood spent on a homestead ranch in cowboy country, near Cody, Wyoming. She told me of trips taken around Yellowstone Park in a covered wagon accompanied by the United States Cavalry. She let me dress up in old clothes found in her dusty attic trunks.

Grandmother Margaret also helped me to build special hideaway places in her backyard, using old quilts draped over my grandfather's wooden lawn chairs. That was the start of my building career. That was also when I began to understand and use my imagination to take me to faraway places and to dream dreams filled with fantastic possibilities. I'm still dreaming today!

This is a book about building things. This is a book about your imagination. It is about imagining things you can build and build-

ing things you can imagine. "But I've never built anything before!" you say. Don't worry. The projects that follow are simple. They don't require many tools, and most of the materials you can find for free, or if you have to buy them they won't cost very much.

This book is also about making special places that are personal, private, and just for you. What can you do in your own hideaway? You might go there to write in your journal or diary, to think, to sing, or maybe to take a nap. Perhaps you could have a sleepover there, read a good book, draw, paint, or write a poem. There are lots of reasons that children and adults like to have a small, cozy space to call their own, and I'm sure you will begin to understand why one is important to you.

In the following chapters you will find some suggestions and directions to build a variety of projects. They include a lean-to,

tepee, tunnel, raft, maze, boxcar, snow fort, and a variety of tents. I encourage you to try some or all of these fun projects, but please don't let your imagination stop there. This is only a starting place. Here are a few other suggestions:

- a fort built out of straw or hay bales
- a tree-less tree house built at the bottom of a tree— or not
- a spaceship made from a refrigerator box rolled into a tube
- a lean-to made of corn- stalks
- an imaginary desert island built in a sandbox
- a fort made with couch cushions
- a lighthouse built with a refrigerator box
- a tent made with saw- horses and a blanket

The materials I have suggested include leaves, sticks, cardboard, string, rope, sheets, blankets, snow, and wooden pallets. The instructions are brief and not too detailed so as to give you room to change things around and find better ways of putting things together. Try to figure things out on your own, but if you get frustrated and can't make something work, ask an adult to help.

By all means, be careful!

Anytime you use tools like hammers, saws, scissors, knives, and pliers, you need to take extra caution. Make sure you know how to use your tools correctly and safely. Ask an adult to show you how to use them the first time and to be on hand each time until the adult feels you are competent. Also, be careful with the materials you will be using. Wood can have splinters; pieces of wire can scratch or prick. And it really hurts if you step on a nail.

One more caution here. NEVER, NEVER use matches, candles, lanterns, or any other source of fire or flame in your hideaway places. If you want artificial light, use a flashlight or battery-powered lantern.

Everyone is born with an imagination and creative abilities. In order to fully use and benefit from this gift, it has to be exercised, just like other parts of your body. I hope this book will help you to exercise your creative spirit, have some fun, learn some new skills, and create some childhood memories of your own.

Good luck and have fun!

Zigzag Pallet Fort

Materials

Pallets (at least 3, as many as you can get!)

Hammer (for removing dangerous nails)

Rope or baling twine (to tie pallets together)

Sheet or tarp (optional)

Paint (optional)

WHAT IS A PALLET? It is a sturdy, portable wooden platform made for storing and moving cargo and freight. Pallets are usually 4 feet square and about 5 inches thick. A small, tractor-like machine called a forklift can pick up heavily loaded pallets and move them easily from place to place. Some pallets have slats on both top and bottom, alternating with empty spaces. Some pallets have a solid top and open bottom. Some are heavier than others. (This is where your grown-up helper comes in handy!)

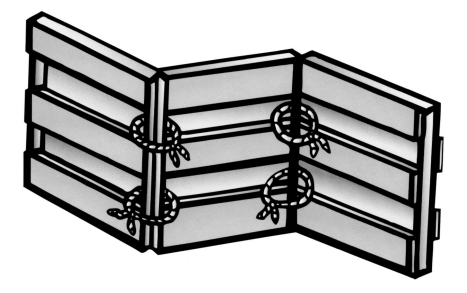

Somewhere in your community you will be able to find some old pallets you can use to build your own special fort. Check with the manager of your local supermarket, chain discount store, or manufacturing plant to see if they will give you some of their discarded pallets. To start this fort you will need at least three, but try to collect a few more if you can. Be sure to ask permission before you take them!

After you have your pallets, check them carefully for loose boards, big splinters, or nails sticking out. For safe playing, pull out the loose nails or pound them back into the boards.

Gather some short pieces of rope (or baling twine, if you know someone who feeds livestock) to use for hinges. Begin to tie the pallets together, end to end. Make your rope hinges tight enough to hold the pallets together but loose enough so the pallets will swing back and forth (like a door on hinges). After you have tied at least three together, ask an adult helper to assist you in standing them up on edge. Position them so they will stand on their own. For instance, with just three pallets tied together, you can make a zigzag wall, a U-shaped hideout, or a small triangular fort.

Each additional pallet you add will increase your options as to how your zigzag fort might be shaped.

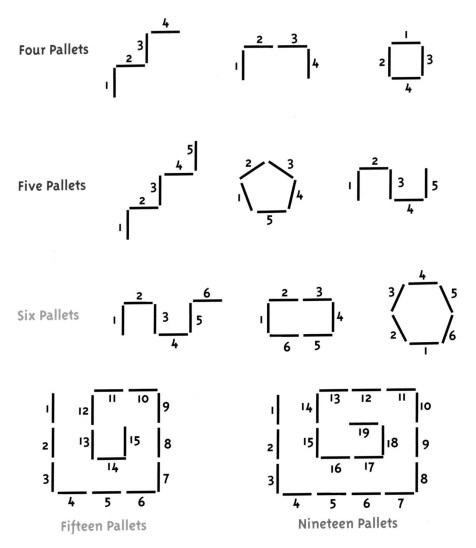

Four Pallets

Five Pallets

Six Pallets

Fifteen Pallets

Nineteen Pallets

If you decide you want to keep out the light or the rain or the neighbors' eyes, you might cover your pallet fort with an old sheet, a tarp, or some tree branches.

Your imagination and a little paint could transform your fort into a log cabin, a fishing shack, or a giant dollhouse.

MASTER FINISHER TIPS

Paint the pallets your favorite colors. For instance, if you imagine you are in a fort, then brown or green paint would make it more realistic. If you are building a maze, any colors you dream up will make it charming and personal.

A-Mazing Tunnel Town

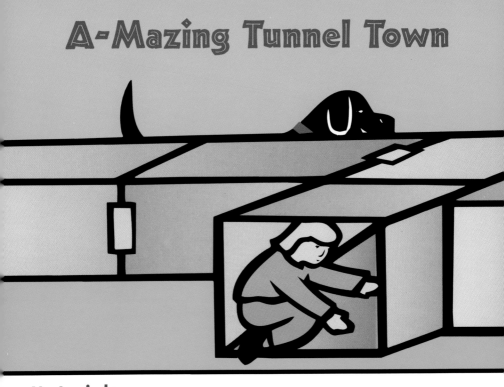

Materials
. . . .

Large cardboard boxes (5–100!)

Knife or scissors **CAUTION!**

Marking pen or poster paints (optional)

Masking tape or duct tape

Book on cave paintings (optional)

HAVE YOU EVER been in a subway tunnel, explored a cave or cavern, been through a mountain or under the water in a tunnel? In the right situation, these can all be exciting places to visit and experience.

Most of us don't have a tunnel in our own backyard, but why not build one for yourself! If you were to grab a shovel and start

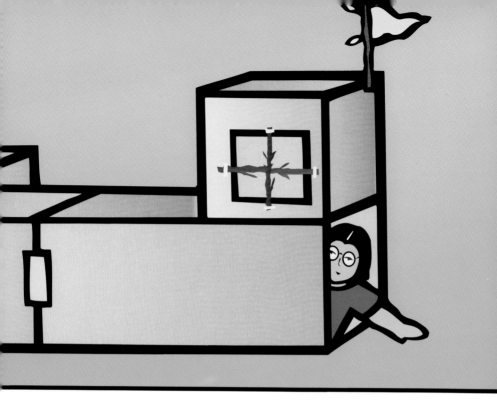

digging, you might meet some resistance (the kind with a tapping toe and a scolding finger). So, let's build an above-ground tunnel or cave.

Go to your local appliance store, chain discount store, or moving company and ask for some old boxes. Tall boxes 3 to 4 feet square would be the best. Refrigerator boxes, washing machine boxes, and wardrobe boxes (from the moving company) will work nicely. The more boxes you get, the larger your tunnel system can be. If you are lucky enough to know someone with a pickup truck, perhaps you could kindly persuade them to help transport your boxes. If not, you may have to carefully fold the boxes flat to get them home, but you can easily put them back together with some masking tape or duct tape. Once the boxes have been reassembled, you are ready to start your tunnel(s).

Lay your boxes out on the ground and decide how you want to join them to shape your tunnel. The boxes can be attached end to end, end to side, in "T" shapes, "S" shapes, and many other forms. You may want to attach a box to the top of your tunnel to use as an entry. Once you have a plan, start connecting boxes to each other. A roll of duct tape will work nicely for this job.

If you have a lot of boxes, you can make a maze to trick your friends. You might create some dead ends, some pop-up spaces, or a few lookout windows for fresh air and light—but just one way out! (Where you intend to crawl through the boxes, of course, leave both ends open.) A knife will work best to cut the cardboard, but you could also use a pair of old scissors. (Be sure to invite an adult helper to be on hand when you cut.) If you use a knife, be especially careful, and always cut away from yourself.

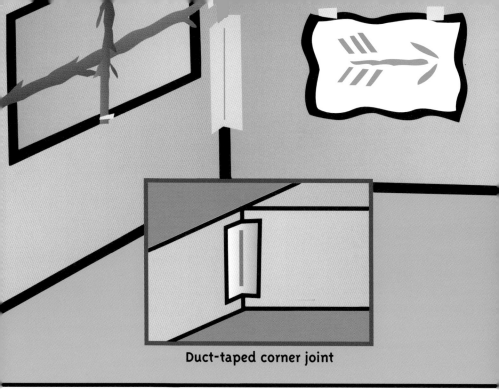

Duct-taped corner joint

You might try a game to see if your friends can find their way through your A-Mazing Tunnel blindfolded! Or, can you think of some fake clues to write inside the tunnel that might trick your friends? Time them: who can find their way out the fastest?

MASTER FINISHER TIPS

Find a book in your library showing ancient cave paintings, and make some similar paintings on the inside of your tunnel/cave. Take your flashlight, explore your tunnel, and imagine you are the first person to discover that part of the world!

Tie-Up Tepee

Materials

6 poles, 1¹/₂ times as tall as yourself

1 shoelace (about 18 inches)

1 sheet, blanket, or plastic tarp

Saw

Drill

Thumb tacks or staples (optional)

LONG AGO BEFORE airplanes, computers, or high-rise buildings, some Native Americans lived in cone-shaped structures called tepees. They were constructed of long, straight poles and covered with animal skins that were sewn together by hand. These homes were

portable. The Indians moved them from place to place—from one hunting ground to the next. Today, some people still use tepees much as a tent would be used. These are especially popular where people want to re-create a feeling of the Old West.

You can build a portable place that resembles a tepee. All you need are 6 poles, a shoelace (about 18 inches long), and some sort of covering, such as an old sheet, blanket (just make sure it's not your mom's heirloom quilt!), or a plastic tarp.

Start by finding your poles. The longer the poles, the bigger your tepee will be. For a personal, one-person space, they should be about 1½ times as tall as you are. You can use wood from a lumberyard (1 x 2s are sturdy enough) or small dead tree limbs 1 to 2 inches in diameter. Don't cut down live trees unless someone gives you permission!

Ask an adult to help you drill a hole near one end of each pole, big enough for the shoelace to slip through. If your poles are "store bought," it won't matter which end you drill. If they are natural poles, they will taper, or grow smaller from one end to the other. Drill the holes on the smaller end.

After the holes are drilled, run the shoelace through all the holes, joining the 6 poles together. Then tie the two ends of the shoelace together.

Now you are ready to raise your tepee. (If you are indoors, set your frame on a rug or carpet to keep it from slipping.) Spread the poles apart at the bottom. Adjust until the 6 poles are balancing steadily. Wrap your covering around the outside of the poles and find a way to attach it. (If you're lucky, the sheet or blanket will hang on all by itself!) Small pieces of string will work nicely. For a more permanent structure, you might use staples or thumbtacks.

If you are working with an adult helper, perhaps you can cut or sew a covering that fits right down over your poles. Be sure to leave an opening for the door.

Invite some friends over to your tepee for a powwow!

MASTER FINISHER TIPS

Paint your tepee cover with Native American symbols. Silhouettes of buffalo, horses, and mountains are a few traditional Native designs.

Huck Finn's Raft

Materials

1 pallet

Thumbtacks or stapler

Boards for rockers (two 1″ x 4″ boards that are 3 feet long, or a similar piece of ¾″ plywood)

Flagpole (broomstick or board 1″x 2″ or 2″x 2″)

Flag material of your choice

Bell or whistle (optional)

Long stick

Nails or screws

Saw

"WE JUDGED THAT three nights more would fetch us to Cairo, at the bottom of Illinois, where the Ohio River comes in and that was what we was after." So thought Huckleberry Finn and his friend Jim as they were floating on their raft down the Mississippi River. Though you may not be able to do that for real, you can sure create an imaginary trip down any river in the world by putting together a few simple items.

Find an old wooden pallet (see page 9 for ideas on finding pallets). The best kind to use for your imaginary raft will be a solid one with no big spaces between the boards. (That way, your feet won't slip through the cracks when the raft rocks back and forth.) This 4´ x 4´ pallet will become your basic raft.

Now, to make it look and feel like a real one. To give your raft a feeling of river motion, you can build some rockers for the bottom.

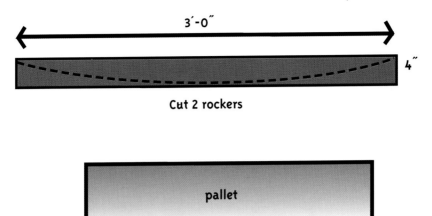

Cut 2 rockers

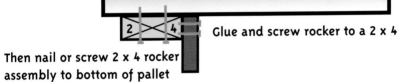

pallet

Glue and screw rocker to a 2 x 4

Then nail or screw 2 x 4 rocker
assembly to bottom of pallet

You need either two 1″ x 4″ boards 3 feet long (or a similar-sized piece of ³/₄″ plywood) to make them from.

CAUTION! You'll probably need an adult to help you cut out the rockers. The pictures show you how to shape them. Screw or nail the rockers to the bottom of your pallet.

Using a scrap piece of cloth or a piece of an old sheet, design a personal flag to fly from your raft. A board 1″ x 2″ or 2″ x 2″, or an old broomstick can be nailed or screwed to the edge of the pallet to carry your flag. Attach the flag to the flagpole with staples or thumbtacks. Find another pole or stick to "pole" your raft along in your imaginary waterway. If you can find an old bicycle horn or bell, attach it somewhere in case you have to send out a signal in the dark or in the fog. You never know what pirates will be roaming the waters!

If you think your legs might get tired on your long river trip, find a stool or an old deck chair to sit on. As you are "floating" along, it might be a good time to go fishing or to read the rest of the *Adventures of Huckleberry Finn.*

CAUTION! Remember, this is not a seaworthy craft, so under no circumstances should you try to float it in a pond, creek, river, pool, or any other body of water. Just "float" it in the sea of grass in your backyard and enjoy the trip.

MASTER FINISHER TIPS

Build side rails from lengths of 2" x 4" board.

Make a fishing pole from a willow branch and string. Tie a small weight, such as a nut from your family's tool chest, to the end of the string for more control of the fishing line.

Backyard Boxcar

Materials

Library book with pictures of trains

2 refrigerator boxes

Sharp knife

Duct tape

Tempera paint

4 small wheels (or extra cardboard to make some) (optional)

6–8 inches of wire (optional)

Stick, large nail, or screw (optional)

HOBOES AND DRIFTERS used to move back and forth across the country by "hopping" a train while it was moving slowly. This was especially popular from the 1920s through the 1940s. The person would ride along on a flatcar or in a boxcar. Though this method of transportation wasn't particularly safe (or legal!), it was seen by many as an exciting and inexpensive way to see the country.

If you think you would like to ride the imaginary rails across the land, why not build your own backyard boxcar? First, go to the library and check out a book on trains so you'll have a good idea what a boxcar looks like. Then stop by your local appliance or chain discount store and ask someone who works there for two refrigerator boxes.

Cut one side out of each box. Attach the two boxes together along the cut edges with duct tape. Cut a couple of round or square holes in the top for light, and cut a door in the side so you can get in and out.

Cutting Cardboard Safely

When using a knife to cut cardboard, there is one way that is safer than all others: work outside on the ground, so the knife enters the dirt with each downward stroke. Cut the cardboard only on your downward strokes. That is, put pressure on the blade when pushing down, but release the pressure when drawing the knife back up. This will prevent the knife from accidentally cutting your arm or leg.

Poke your knife into the cardboard where you want to start the cut. Then kneel down at least two feet behind the knife. Lean up on your free hand, keeping that hand well away from the cutting line. This position will give you "leverage" (allow you to be in control of the knife!).

Once you have finished cutting on one line, remove the knife, turn your body, and start again on another line. Remember— for good control, you should always have the knife out in front of you, not to the side. And your free hand should be well away from the blade.

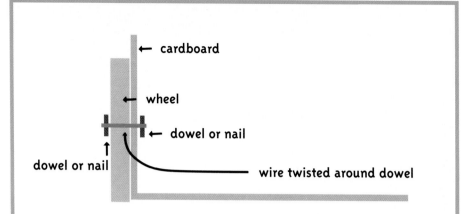

← cardboard

← wheel

← dowel or nail

dowel or nail

wire twisted around dowel

MASTER FINISHER TIPS

If you can find some old lawn-mower or wagon wheels, attach them to the sides to make your boxcar look authentic. If you can't find any, perhaps you can cut some out of cardboard. Since your boxcar won't actually be rolling along the rails, you can attach your wheels to the sides of the cardboard with some short pieces of wire. Twist the wire around a wooden dowel or long nail. Push both ends of the wire through your wheel, then push both ends through the boxcar. On the inside, twist the wire ends around a stick, large nail, or screw. Turn the stick clockwise, winding the wire around it until the stick is next to the inside wall of the boxcar. This should hold it in place.

Buy some tempera paint or find some old paint around the house (remember your manners—ask before taking!) and paint your cardboard boxcar to look like the real thing. Don't forget to name your railroad line and paint your car number on the side.

Now load your boxcar with an old chair, your lunch, and a radio or a good book. Spend some time there alone or with a friend, traveling the rails of the world.

Rustic Lean-To

Attach covering to 2 x 4 or pole

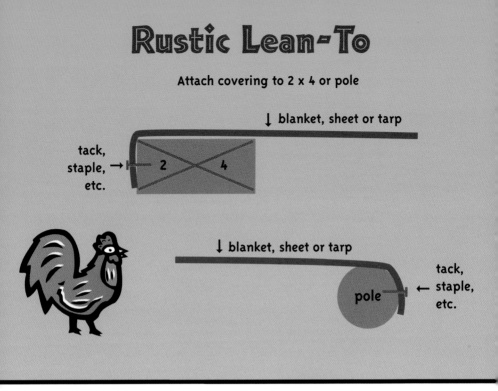

↓ blanket, sheet or tarp

tack, staple, etc. →

2   4

↓ blanket, sheet or tarp

pole

tack, staple, etc. ←

Materials

(2) 8-foot 2 x 4s

Blanket, sheet, or tarp

Thumbtacks, carpet tacks, or staple gun

Hammer (if using carpet tacks)

Saw   **CAUTION!**

WOULD YOU LIKE a special place that you can build quickly without too many materials? Would you like one that you can move around and use over and over again?

Here's an idea for a simple hideaway that you can easily move from place to place. Get two 2 x 4s eight feet long. (You could instead use two poles you find on the ground in the woods.) Find an

old blanket, sheet, or plastic tarp and spread it out on the ground. Lay the 2 x 4s along two opposite edges of the tarp. If you want a taller, narrower shelter, place the poles along the long edges. If you want a shorter, wider shelter, place the poles along the short edges. If your covering happens to be square, it doesn't matter!

Using thumbtacks, carpet tacks, or a heavy-duty staple gun, attach your covering material to the poles. Then saw off the ends of the poles so they are even with the corners of your covering.

When you are ready to set up your hideaway, just "lean" the two poles up against a house, a barn, a shed, or anything else that can become the vertical side (that's the straight up-and-down side) of your lean-to. (Don't lean it against something that might walk away!)

When you have finished hiding out for the day, your lean-to can be rolled around the two poles and stored in your closet or in the garage.

In a pinch, you can build an open-sided lean-to by stretching a very tight rope between two trees. Attach your covering to the pole or rope, and stake the other end to the ground. This can provide a quickly built shelter to sleep under in your yard or in the woods.

MASTER FINISHER TIPS

You can make your lean-to look more rustic, more like it belongs to nature. Gather enough fallen tree branches to cover up the tarp. (This could be especially fun when you go on a camping trip.) If dead leaves are still clinging to the branches, so much the better. Once your lean-to has been leaned against a wall, lean the branches over it to hide the tarp from view. This will camouflage your hideaway, making it a place where you can plan secret missions and keep a quiet lookout for spies!

Chicken-Wire Hut

Materials

30 or more feet of chicken wire, 4 to 6 feet wide

(6–7) 1˝ wooden dowels

Yardstick or measuring tape

Tin snips or old scissors **CAUTION!**

1 small roll of thin wire or string

HERE'S A PROJECT you can build with a pile of fall leaves, old grass clippings, sticks you pick up around the yard or in the woods, or branches from trees that have been trimmed or clipped. (Don't cut living tree branches unless you have permission.)

Either find or buy at least 30 feet of chicken wire. Chicken wire

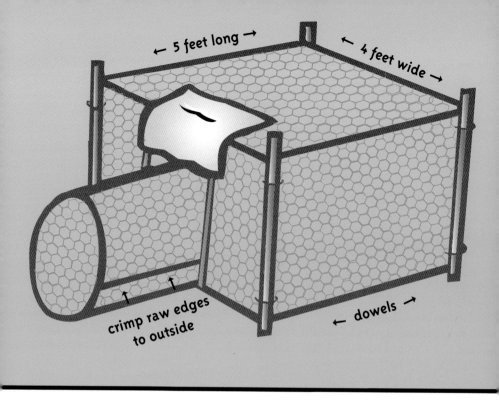

← 5 feet long →

← 4 feet wide →

crimp raw edges to outside

← dowels →

can be purchased in rolls at hardware or farm supply stores. (Or you might be able to bargain with a neighbor who has part of a roll left over from some project.) Chicken wire is light and flexible, and can be easily cut, formed, and shaped. It comes in different sizes—that is, different widths with different sizes of holes. A width at least 4 feet will make a roomy hut. Holes 1 to 2 inches across would work best, but if what you have on hand is larger, go ahead and use that.

First, choose a spot to build your hut, then pound 4 dowels into the ground for the corner posts. Position the dowels about 4 to 5 feet apart for the length of your hut. The width of the hut should be no wider than the *width* of your chicken wire. In the center of the front end of your rectangle, pound in 2 more dowels. Leave a space between these 2 dowels wide enough for you to fit through. These will frame the doorway.

Measure the distance all the way around the outside of your rectangle. Unroll the wire; measure off enough to match your perimeter measurement. (The perimeter is the outside!) You will need some tin snips or old scissors to cut the chicken wire. (Uh, *uh*, UH! Don't use Mom's good scissors—it will make them dull.)

 Cut off the wire at this spot. (This might be a job for Super . . . *adult helper!*)

Wrap the wire around the outside of the rectangle, starting at one side of the door and ending at the other side. Secure the chicken wire to each dowel with string or thin wire as you go along. When you get to the other side of the door, wrap any extra wire around to the inside. Carefully bend those loose ends through to the outside so they can't scratch you when you're playing inside.

Next, cut a length of chicken wire to make a roof. Lay it over the top of your hut and attach it to the walls.

Now cut enough wire to make a round tunnel large enough to crawl through. Slide the tunnel into position between the two dowels that mark the doorway. (This tunnel entrance keeps big people out!) You could either leave the space above the tunnel open for a window, or you could hang a towel over it.

After you have built your wire form, it's time to give your hut personality! Gather colorful autumn leaves, grass clippings, sticks, brush, or other natural material you might find. ("Light" is a key word here. If the materials are too heavy, they might cave in the wire form.) Begin piling some on the roof, and attach some as you can to the sides.

When you are finished, you should have something that looks just like a big pile of stuff on the outside. But there will be a cozy hideaway on the inside. Enjoy your natural hut, and remember that the covering is dry and flammable. If you want some light inside, use a flashlight. NEVER, NEVER use a match, candle, lantern, or anything else with flame in a hut.

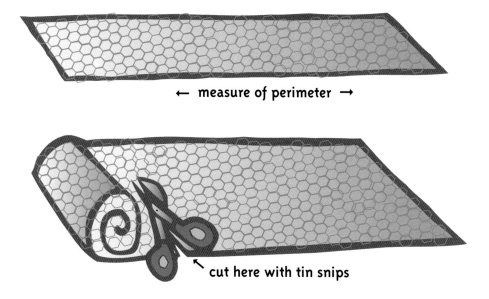

← measure of perimeter →

cut here with tin snips

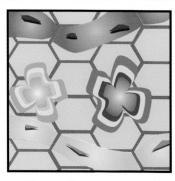

MASTER FINISHER TIPS

You could change your hut by making coverings other than natural materials. Here are some ideas to get you started:

Weave strips of crepe paper or fabric in and out of the holes to turn it into a bright, cheerful clubhouse.

Twist flowers out of paper towels, tissue paper, or crepe paper. Stuff these into the holes (from the outside!) to make your hut look like a parade float.

For a space-age look, buy three or four rolls of heavy-duty aluminum foil. Cut the foil into squares about twice as big as the holes in your chicken wire. Poke the foil into the holes from the outside, molding each piece to the wire until it holds.

Molded-Snow Fort

Materials
· · · · · · · · · · · · · · · ·

SNOW!—lots of it

2 ¹/₂-gallon bucket

Tamping tool (optional)

Large spoon

Poster paints (optional)

PVC pipe (about 2 feet, optional)

12″ – 14″

HERE'S A FORT that you will be able to build only if Mother Nature cooperates by providing you with her most delightful construction material—snow! Any amount will do, but the deeper it is, the easier it will be to construct this fort. (If there are only a couple inches of

snow on the ground, you might have to travel around the neighbor-hood to gather enough to make a fort!)

The first step is to decide what you want your fort to look like and where to build it. Snow is a tremendously sculptural material. With a little work, you can make this fort look like just about anything. It can be round, square, rectangular, triangular, or free-form. Mark off the walls in the snow. The number of snowballs or snow blocks you'll need depends on what size fort you want to build. (This might be a good time to enlist recruits!)

There are two ways to make your chilly building blocks. The first is simply to make a big batch of snowballs 12 to 14 inches in diameter—about the size of a basketball. (If you make them much bigger, you might not be able to lift them off the ground!

Hummm . . . maybe this is a job for an adult helper!) Place them edge to edge along the outline you marked off. Rest the second layer of snowballs atop the cracks between those in the first layer. Pat them in place just hard enough to make them stick to the row beneath (but not so hard you knock them to pieces!) Continue in layers until the fort is as high as you want it—but not higher than your shoulders. You don't want the snow to bury you (or maybe your little brother or the dog) if the fort falls down.

The second method is to mold building blocks that are uniform in size and shape. Find a 2 1/2-gallon galvanized bucket. (Yes, your mom's plastic cleaning bucket will work just fine—be sure to ask her if you can borrow it.) Set your bucket outside till it is as cold as the snow so your snow bricks won't stick to the bucket. Then shovel it full of snow and pack it down with your hands, the end of the shovel, or a small wooden block. (If your boot is smaller than a 2 1/2-gallon size, you can even tamp it with your foot!)

Turn the bucket upside down on the mark that outlines your fort. Tap the bucket on the bottom and the snow block should fall out. (You might have to give it a good whack!) Continue to mold bucket snow bricks until you have lined the edge of your fort. When you start on the next layer, set the bucket over the crack between the two bricks below it, like the picture above shows. This will make your fort stronger and more stable than stacking one brick directly on top of another.

If you decide you want a roof on your fort, use an old blanket, sheet, or plastic tarp.

Enjoy your fort while you can because you never know how long it will last.

MASTER FINISHER TIPS

You may want to leave spaces for a door and dome windows while you are building, but because snow is so easily shaped you can also decide later and cut openings out of your walls. A big spoon would be a good carving tool. Be sure to ask before you borrow.

On the inside of the fort, you can pack snow to make benches and tables. Or you can hollow out a place to hold a flashlight or a warm drink.

Design a flag to decorate your fort. Attach the flag to a length of PVC pipe, then stick the pipe into the top layer of the fort wall.

Color your fort with dry-powder poster paint—the kind your teacher uses at school to make finger paint. Put a little powder in your hand and sprinkle it over the area you want to color.

Terrific Tents

Materials

Blanket, sheet, or tarp

1 long stick

2 sturdy chairs

Some heavy books

Clothesline rope (outdoor option)

2 towels (optional)

Hammer (outdoor option)

TENTS, TENTS, TENTS—there are all kinds of tents. There are wall tents, pup tents, dome tents, one-person tents, ten-person tents, canvas tents, nylon tents, round tents, square tents, tall tents, short tents, waterproof tents, and some that leak. A tent is made from

some sort of covering, such as canvas, animal skins, or synthetic cloth, stretched over a frame made of wood or metal or rope.

If you are inside on a rainy day and want to make believe you are on a backcountry expedition in Yellowstone Park or camping next to the Amazon River, you can make a temporary tent with a blanket or sheet, a long stick, a couple of chairs, and some heavy books.

Find 2 sturdy, straight-backed chairs and place them back-to-back 5 or 6 feet apart. Make sure they are stable and won't fall over easily. Then get a long stick and rest it on the backs of the chairs. This will be the "ridgepole" of your tent. You may want to tie the pole to the backs of the chairs to keep it from slipping. (If you are using Mom's good chairs, be careful not to scratch them.) Now, drape an old blanket, sheet, or canvas drop cloth over the ridgepole with half of the covering on each side of the pole. Stretch out the covering so there is space underneath the pole. Place some books or other heavy objects on the edges of the tent material to hold it in position. If you want privacy, hang a towel over the open ends of your tent, or stack some pillows or cushions there.

A similar tent can be constructed outdoors, and if you get permission, maybe you can even plan to sleep out in it. Stretch clothesline rope between two trees to make your ridgepole. If trees aren't available, use what is—heavy lawn furniture, porch posts, clothesline poles, etc. For a waterproof tent, stretch plastic tarp over the ridgepole.

Make some tent stakes out of sticks or pieces of dead wood. Hammer them into the ground, then tie the edges of the tarp to them with pieces of sturdy string or rope. If you are using a blanket or sheet, you can knot the corners in order to have something to which you can tie your stake lines. If you plan to spend the night, you might want to put a piece of plastic on the ground before you put down your blankets or sleeping bag—and don't forget your flashlight.

This tent will keep out a gentle rain, but it won't protect you from mosquitoes!

MASTER FINISHER TIPS

Staking a tent is a skill that every camper should learn. Your stake can be a sturdy stick, or it can be a plastic or metal variety from a sporting-goods store.

With a little practice, you can balance the tension between the ground stake and the tent loops (or ropes) for maximum staying power. Depending on whether the ground is hard or soft, dry or muddy, you might need to test a couple of positions for the stake.

First, put your stake through the loop. Then use the stake to pull the loop away from the tent, creating tautness. Poke the stake into the ground at an angle, with the tip that goes into the ground pointing toward the tent. The top points away from the tent. Use a hammer to pound the stake in place. If you have found a solid spot, the stake will hold its position, even in a wind—and even if someone trips over the stake!

Open-Air Big Top

Materials

Large tarp or sheets sewn together

40–75 feet of sturdy rope

4–8 wooden or plastic stakes

Long center pole (optional)

Flat cardboard, enough to equal outside measurement of tarp (optional)

Duct tape (if using cardboard)

Poster paints (optional)

Hammer

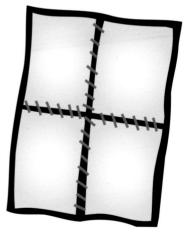

Sheets sewn together

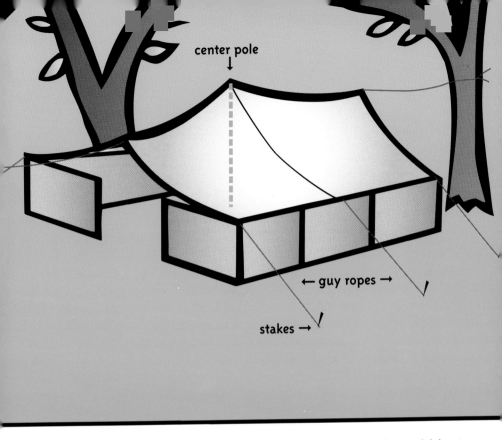

center pole
↓

← guy ropes →

stakes →

HAVE YOU EVER dreamed that the Greatest Show on Earth could be in your very own backyard, complete with interesting animals, clowns, acrobats, and, of course, a big circus tent? Why not gather some of your friends and create your own circus in the backyard?

First, make your own "big top." You'll need to find some material to use as the tent covering. The larger the material, the larger your tent will be. Perhaps you can get a very large plastic tarp, or maybe each of your friends could contribute one or two old sheets; then one of your parents could sew them together.

To set up the big top, first stretch a rope tightly between two trees, two buildings, or two clothesline poles. (Clothesline rope is probably too flimsy for this project because it will stretch under the weight of the tent.) Tie the rope high enough to support the ridge of your circus tent—that is, high enough for you and all your friends to stand under it! (An adult helper with a stepladder would be an ideal resource about now.) Stretch your material over the ridgeline and tie a rope about 4 or 5 feet long to each corner of the top.

Next, find some wooden stakes (or use plastic tent stakes—they have handy hooks!). Secure the rope at each corner of the top to one of the stakes. Stretch out the top and pound the stakes into the ground (angled away from the ridge—otherwise they'll keep popping out of the ground and you'll have a circus putting up the big top!). If the top is very large, you may need to add a ground stake or two between the corner stakes.

Putting a Peak on Your Tent

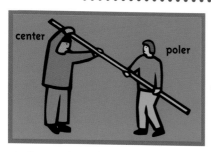

Erecting the center pole takes teamwork because the pole is often too long for one person to handle. First, figure out where the center of your tent top is. One person should stand right under the center. The other person, the "poler," should bring the long pole inside, under the tent, handing the top end of the pole to the "center" buddy. The "center" points the pole upward, moving his or her hands down the pole to balance it while the "poler" slowly walks closer and closer to the center. As the top of the pole reaches the tent covering overhead, it will push the covering up in the center, making a lot more room underneath. When the "poler" has come face-to-face with the "center," the two should rest the bottom of the pole on the ground. The weight of the tent covering resting on it will be enough to hold it in place.

MASTER FINISHER TIPS

Paint the cardboard outside with circus scenes and your favorite circus animals. Inside, why not paint crowds of people sitting in bleacher stands?

If you want your big top to have a center peak, you'll need to find a pole that is a foot or two higher than your ridgeline.Carefully push the pole up in the center of your tent. Be careful not to rip the covering material when erecting the peak pole. Now that your basic tent top is in place, you can choose either to leave it an "open-air" tent or to create sides with a number of large cardboard boxes (bicycle boxes would be ideal), opened out flat. You'll need as much cardboard as it will take to run it around the perimeter (that's all along the outside edge) of your tent. Attach the boxes to the lower edges of your tent covering with duct tape.

Now that you have a circus tent, you and your friends can dress yourselves up and imagine that you are clowns, jugglers, acrobats, or trapeze artists. Maybe you could use stuffed animals for tigers or bears (or dress up your little brother!). Get some mats or a few folding chairs, place them under the big top, and let the show begin!

Other Activity Books from

Gibbs Smith Junior

COOKING ON A STICK

Campfire Recipes for Kids
by Linda White
illustrated by Fran Lee
$8.95

SLEEPING IN A SACK

Camping Activities for Kids
by Linda White
illustrated by Fran Lee
$10.00

Available at bookstores or order directly from the publisher.
GIBBS SMITH PUBLISHER 1.800.748.5439
www.Gibbs-Smith.com

I.S. 61 Library

S. 61 Library

I.S. 61 Library